SandCastle™

Animal Homes

Home
Sweet
Burrow

Mary Elizabeth Salzmann

CONSULTING EDITOR, DIANE CRAIG, M.A./READING SPECIALIST

A Division of ABDO
ABDO
Publishing Company

visit us at www.abdopublishing.com

Published by ABDO Publishing Company, a division of ABDO, P.O. Box 398166, Minneapolis, Minnesota 55439.

Printed in the United States of America, North Mankato, Minnesota
062011
092011

 PRINTED ON RECYCLED PAPER

Editor: Katherine Hengel
Content Developer: Nancy Tuminelly
Cover and Interior Design and Production: Anders Hanson, Mighty Media, Inc.
Photo Credits: Shutterstock

Library of Congress Cataloging-in-Publication Data
Salzmann, Mary Elizabeth, 1968-
  Home sweet burrow / Mary Elizabeth Salzmann.
     p. cm. -- (Animal homes)
  ISBN 978-1-61714-815-6
  1. Burrowing animals--Juvenile literature. 2. Animals--Habitations--Juvenile literature. I. Title.
QL756.15.S25 2012
591.56′4--dc22
                         2010053037

SANDCASTLE™ LEVEL: TRANSITIONAL

SandCastle™ books are created by a team of professional educators, reading specialists, and content developers around five essential components—phonemic awareness, phonics, vocabulary, text comprehension, and fluency—to assist young readers as they develop reading skills and strategies and increase their general knowledge. All books are written, reviewed, and leveled for guided reading, early reading intervention, and Accelerated Reader® programs for use in shared, guided, and independent reading and writing activities to support a balanced approach to literacy instruction. The SandCastle™ series has four levels that correspond to early literacy development. The levels are provided to help teachers and parents select appropriate books for young readers.

Emerging Readers
(no flags)

Beginning Readers
(1 flag)

Transitional Readers
(2 flags)

Fluent Readers
(3 flags)

Contents

What Is a Burrow?

A burrow is a tunnel or hole dug by an animal. Burrows can be in sand, dirt, wood, or rock.

A burrow can be a single small hole. Or it can be made up of many long, **connecting** tunnels.

5

Animals and Burrows

Burrows **protect** animals from bad weather. Animals also go into their burrows to hide from **predators**.

Meerkats live in burrows.

Meerkats dig large burrows that have many tunnels and **entrances**. Meerkats take turns standing guard. The guard barks to **warn** the others of danger. Then all the meerkats run into the burrow.

Moles live in burrows.

Moles dig burrows that have many tunnels and rooms. They eat worms and bugs that they find underground. Moles **rarely** leave their burrows.

Fiddler crabs live in burrows.

Fiddler crabs live on beaches. They dig burrows in the sand. During high **tide**, each crab covers its burrow **entrance** with sand. This keeps air in and water out.

Bee-eaters live in burrows.

Bee-eaters dig burrows in dirt or sand. Some bee-eater burrows are in the ground. Others are in cliffs or **riverbanks**.

European rabbits live in burrows.

European rabbits dig burrows with many tunnels. Up to 20 rabbits can live in a burrow. They **usually** stay in their burrows during the day. They leave the burrow at night to find food.

Burrowing owls live in burrows.

Burrowing owls **usually** use burrows dug by other animals. But they can dig their own if necessary. They line their burrows with droppings from animals such as cows and horses.

Groundhogs live in burrows.

Groundhogs dig their burrows near forests. In the summer they leave the burrow during the day to eat. They **hibernate** in their burrows during the winter.

Could *you* live
in a burrow?

Quiz

1. Animals do not go into their burrows to hide from **predators**. *True or false?*

2. Moles often leave their burrows. *True or false?*

3. European rabbits stay in their burrows during the night. *True or false?*

4. Burrowing owls **usually** use burrows dug by other animals. *True or false?*

5. Groundhogs **hibernate** in their burrows during the winter. *True or false?*

Glossary

connect – to join two or more things together.

entrance – a door or a way in.

hibernate – to pass the winter in a deep sleep.

predator – an animal that hunts others.

protect – to guard someone or something from harm or danger.

rarely – not very often.

riverbank – the ground along the side of a river.

tide – change in sea level.

usually – commonly or normally.

warn – to tell others that danger is near.